Beyond Blame

Distributed by Publishers Group West

Beyond Blame

Blame

A FULL-RESPONSIBILITY APPROACH TO LIFE

YEHUDA BERG

For further information:

The Kabbalah Centre
155 E. 48th St., New York, NY 10017
1062 S. Robertson Blvd, Los Angeles, CA 90035

1.800.Kabbalah www.kabbalah.com

First Edition
November 2006
Printed in USA
ISBN10: 1-57189-545-0
ISBN13: 978-1-57189-545-5

Design: HL Design (Hyun Min Lee) www.hldesignco.com

DEDICATION

This is dedicated to my young friend Yoni who left this world this year at the young age of 19. In your absence, all those whose lives you have touched have chosen to use your passing as an opportunity to share and help others.

You have been an inspiration to so many to go beyond blame and find happiness and Light amidst what could have been incomprehensible darkness and suffering. Thank you for your gift. May your soul delight in the giving you have created.

TABLE OF CONTENTS

ACKNOWLEDGMENTS

To the people who make my life better each and every day: my parents, the Rav and Karen; my brother Michael; my wife Michal and our children; and my dear friend Billy.

PROLOGUE

July 9, 2006, was an amazing day in human history. For a few brief hours, billions of people were intensely focused on one event. Nothing like this had ever happened before. The first moon walk, the resignation of President Richard Nixon, not even the final episode of *American Idol* had attracted such a gigantic audience. The event was the final game of the 2006 World Cup soccer tournament, watched by a huge percentage of the world's total population, on millions of television screens.

A much smaller number, of course, were actually present at the game—and I was one of them. Soccer had never really been my favorite sport, but when a ticket suddenly became available, I couldn't resist the chance to attend the biggest sports event ever. Not only did it turn out to be a great game, but it was also a perfect metaphor for the ideas you'll encounter in this book.

Even if you don't pay any attention to sports, you probably know that the French star Zinedine Zidane was ejected in the final minutes of the World Cup championship game for suddenly head-butting Marco Materazzi, an Italian defensive player. When I saw this with my own eyes, my first response was complete disbelief. How could one of the world's greatest and most experienced players commit such a blatant foul at the most critical moment of his career, with billions of people watching? It cost Zidane's team the game, and it became the defining moment of his career.

Although like everyone else I was mystified at first, I think I understand what happened on that soccer field. While Zinedine Zidane's action seemed shocking at the time, the truth is millions of people do the same thing every day.

You see, the blatant foul by the French soccer star might have been a surprise to the spectators, and it might even have surprised Zidane himself, but I don't think it was a surprise to his opponents on the Italian team. I think it was exactly what they planned, what they expected, and what they brought about.

"This guy Zidane is a great player, and we might not be able to beat him on the field," they might have said. "But maybe we can get him off the field. In fact, maybe we can get him to *take himself* off the field. All we have to do is figure out something that will get him to go out of control and react without thinking."

And that's what they did.

No one knows exactly what the Italian player said that caused Zidane to do something crazy and throw away the chance of a lifetime. That detail doesn't really matter anyway, since what affects a French soccer star may not be the same thing that would affect you or me. But the important point is this: there *are* things that will cause you to react suddenly in ways that are totally against your best interests. There are things that will make you *take yourself* right out of the game—not the game of soccer, but the game of achieving your purpose in life.

And there is even an Opponent who is concentrating on exactly how to push your very specific hot buttons. As you'll learn in these pages, one of the most potent of those buttons is called BLAME. When you react to that button, you destroy your own chances of getting what you really want. But if you *resist* and *restrict* your reaction, you can win the game—and for you it's a lot bigger game than even the World Cup soccer final.

Please read this book very carefully. When you take these lessons to heart, I promise you that your life will be transformed for the better. So when you're ready, turn the page. The game of *your* lifetime is about to begin.

Part One

BEYOND BLAME

You're on the telephone, and you've been waiting on hold for a very long time. Suddenly you hear a click, followed by a pre-recorded voice saying, "If you'd like to make a call, please hang up and dial again."

You're sitting in your car at a traffic light, late for an important meeting. The guy in the car in front of you doesn't see the light change because he's busy with his cell phone, and when you honk he doesn't move.

It's your birthday, and your significant other has forgotten the date.

All kinds of upsetting things happen every day. And sometimes real catastrophes strike—Hurricane Katrina, 9/11, a divorce, a death. When these things occur, you might ask yourself, *"Why do these things happen?"*

The answer may surprise you:

It's God's fault!

In 1970, Russel T. Tansie, an Arizona lawyer, filed a $100,000 damage suit against God on behalf of his secretary, Betty Penrose, who accused God of negligence in His power over the weather when He allowed a lightning bolt to strike her home. Ms. Penrose won the case when the defendant failed to appear in court. Whether or not she collected is not a matter of record.

There's only one problem with blaming everything on God. *YOU are God*. You just don't know it yet.

The subject of this book is BEYOND BLAME—what lies on the other side of the "life is happening to *me*" syndrome or the blame game. This book is about how to generate for yourself the total, overwhelming joy that comes from being the Creator of your emotions, your thoughts, and ultimately, of your life as a whole.

So let's be very clear. You may think you've picked up some sort of self-help book here. Well, it will help—why else would I have written it?—but not in the way you think. First off, by reading this book, you will connect to a source of energy that will give you the power and courage to stop blaming and to start creating the life you want. I'll be the first to admit that when you blame someone for the things that go wrong in your life, it feels good. But that warm feeling doesn't last. Ultimately, you will find yourself alone with your issues, blaming someone or something else for the fact that you are unhappy. Still, the lure of that feeling is so strong that even long-time students of Kabbalah forget that the relief we get from blaming is only temporary. No matter how familiar you are with these concepts, this book serves as a reminder.

A QUICK KABBALAH QUIZ

Q: What is happiness?
A: Happiness is the outcome of taking responsibility.

Q: What is ultimate happiness?
A: Ultimate happiness is taking ultimate responsibility.

Whoa! Wait a minute. Ultimate responsibility? I thought happiness came from getting something I want, or eating my favorite meal, or having the woman or man I have been thinking about at the office, pay attention to me.

Ultimate responsibility—that doesn't seem like happiness—that seems like a lot of hard work.

Please pay careful attention here. According to Kabbalah, happiness comes from accepting your responsibilities—and your ultimate responsibility is to be happy! This is not just some kind of circular reasoning, because the happiness we refer to does not consist simply of momentary feelings of pleasure. It is the sustained happiness, the joy, the total fulfillment that comes from connecting to the Source of All Happiness —which kabbalists call the Light.

And where does that Light reside? Right inside each one of us.

HEAVEN ON EARTH (ALMOST)

According to Kabbalah, there really was a time when we "had it all." More precisely, we were *given* it all: total fulfillment was bestowed on us by the Creator, who—like a parent granting a child's every wish—only wanted us to be happy.

The only thing we did not have was the opportunity to be in charge of our own destiny, to develop our own self-worth, to earn our own success, to be the source of our own joy. In other words, we weren't the *Cause* of our happiness; we were the *Effect* of the Creator's desire to make us happy.

It turns out that happiness was and is the one thing that nobody, not even the Creator of the universe, could give us.

Imagine, for a moment, your own version of paradise. It doesn't have to be the biblical Garden of Eden. Forget about the animals and forbidden fruit. Just picture an environment in which you're given everything you could possibly want. You're handed an attractive, healthy body; all the money you'll ever need or want; a loving partner; creative projects; well-behaved, smart children.

It's a great feeling, right? But even in this paradise, the truth is there will *always* be something you lack or something more you want. That's simply human nature.

Why is it human nature?

THE ANSWER TO THAT IS . . .

There was a place called the Endless World, filled with God's infinite Light—brighter than a thousand suns—and overflowing with total abundance. The Light was the source of infinite peace, love, health, sustenance, well-being, and all manner of true fulfillment.

The inherent nature of the Creator was the quality of endless sharing. But in the Endless World, there was no one with whom to share this boundless fulfillment. So God created a vessel—humanity—whose sole nature was the desire to receive. And thus there was perfect balance: the Light shared and the vessel received.

Then a profound transformation began to take place. Just as a cup gets warm when hot liquid is poured into it, the vessel of humankind began to absorb the qualities of the Light. In addition to the desire to receive, the vessel of humanity now embodied the Creator's desire to share, to initiate, and to create.

Once it was imbued with the nature of the Creator, the vessel felt unfulfilled by all the abundance it had been spoon-fed. Kabbalists call this condition *Bread of Shame.* As a result, the vessel chose to pull back from the primordial paradise to find its own way to fulfillment: *"Don't fulfill my desire unless I have earned it!"* This action was the impetus for the creation of this physical world, where we, as humanity can only derive true fulfillment and true happiness—the kind we did not have in the Endless World—through the work of becoming like the Creator. Only when we initiate, share, create, and take charge can we draw the Light into our lives and achieve the fulfillment we truly want.

ASK YOURSELF HONESTLY:
"WHAT DO I REALLY WANT?"

Many people tell themselves, "If I could just make a little more money . . .," or "If I could just get a better job
. . .," or "If I could just get along better with my spouse
. . .," or maybe "If I could just get out of this apartment
and into a nice house . . . then everything would be all
right and I would be happy." But we know that those
things don't make us happy. Sure, they may give us
some pleasure temporarily. But our problems don't go
away.

Many struggling people believe that winning the lottery
would solve all their problems and make them happy.
Well, the rent would be covered, you could pay off that
credit card debt, and you could buy all those things you
want without worrying about the prices, but could
money cure your friend's terminal cancer? Could it
bring you your soul mate? Could it make your children
love you? Could it fill the empty pit inside that whispers
in the dark of night, "Is this all there is?"

Stories about lottery winners, after the first flush of victory, rarely end happily. No matter how many houses and cars and digital gizmos winners can now buy, their winnings can't protect them from isolation, depression, or death. And the way in which they received their wealth didn't increase their self-worth or their ability to create or share. It's Bread of Shame.

The Creator made this universe for us so we could achieve the only form of happiness we really desire, the only thing that we did not have before—the ability to create our own satisfaction. There is no one else in the world who can completely fulfill our desires for us. That's the bottom line: one person cannot give another person the joy of self-attainment. And self-attainment is the only way we can have the complete contentment we desire. As the ancient kabbalists teach us, it is part of human nature and the nature of this world that no matter how much is given to us, as long as we are the ones who are receiving and not the ones who are giving, we will always feel Bread of Shame. We will always be the vessel and not the Creator. We will always feel powerless. We will always find someone to blame for our unhappiness.

You know the saying that happiness is a choice. Well, according to Kabbalah, happiness is actually the *result* of the countless choices that we make at every moment. From a kabbalistic viewpoint, it is not the *rightness* of a choice that matters, it is just that in making a conscious choice, we move ourselves beyond the possibility of blaming, toward the certainty of true happiness.

If we are not aware of the constant choices that we make, then we eventually become controlled by outside forces or random situations and feel powerless in a universe that is chaotically happening *to us.*

The truth is, when we are really aware of ourselves, we see that we are always making choices, although the choices may be made unconsciously. Even deciding to postpone making a choice—or not making one at all— is in fact a choice in itself.

It may sound like a tall order to be conscious of and responsible for our choices, but it is possible. When we decide that we want to get rid of blame, anger, frustration, envy, bitterness, regret, guilt, and a thousand other negative feelings that are poisoning our life right now, then we can begin to write the screenplay for the life we want to live.

Part Two

THE TECHNOLOGY
TO GO BEYOND
BLAME

If you've heard it said that Kabbalah is a religion, please let go of that thought right now. Kabbalah is a results-oriented system that explains the laws of the universe and how we can best operate within it.

Kabbalah doesn't intellectualize or rationalize. Kabbalah is infinitely practical—a time-tested *technology* designed to give us the tools to access the energy we need and want from the source of that energy. In a sense, it's like going to a website and downloading a song. Kabbalah shows us how to download from the *99 Percent Realm*, where all happiness resides, where true friendship and love exist, where all sustenance, prosperity, and fulfillment dwell.

THE 99 PERCENT WORLD

Kabbalists refer to the physical world—the world we know through touch, taste, sight, sound, and smell—as the *1 Percent Reality*. The immeasurably larger domain, the remaining *99 Percent*, is hidden from our everyday awareness.

The 99 Percent World is not something you can measure with a yardstick, clock, or thermometer, even though it's always there. Think of a lamp. Although the light may be very bright and powerful, when a blanket is placed on top of it, it's as if the light had disappeared. Kabbalah teaches that the Creator's Light is hidden from us not by one blanket, but by ten intervening dimensions, like curtains hung between us and the Light and us. Whenever one of your dreams comes true, whenever you have a problem for which a solution suddenly appears, whenever you bump into the very person you were just thinking about, you have connected with the 99 Percent World.

The 99 Percent is the ultimate source of joy, waiting for us to connect with it.

Why do we have to connect with it? Why isn't it just available to us?

Remember, humanity was unfulfilled by just receiving the Light passively. We felt powerless. We wanted to do away with Bread of Shame by giving rather than just receiving. We wanted to earn our happiness through our spiritual work—the work of drawing down the Light from the 99 Percent World, and then behaving like the Light by sharing and caring for others.

THE OPPONENT

So our purpose in life is to become the Creator of our own ultimate happiness, and we need to do this as a matter of choice (free will). But how can we make a positive choice without the possibility of making a negative one? Part of our spiritual work is to overcome the force that leads us in the opposite direction, which Kabbalah calls the Opponent.

There is a story in *The Zohar*, the foundational text of Kabbalah, about a great king who was ready to step down from the throne. He wanted his son to succeed him as king, so he decided to test his son's character. He asked the most beautiful harlot in all the land to use her many charms to seduce his son. The son refused her advances and the king happily turned over the reign of his kingdom. *The Zohar* asks: Who was responsible for the boy becoming king? It was the harlot, acting as his Opponent. Had he not had the opportunity to be tested, the son would not have risen to the stature of king.

The Opponent is both external and internal. The external force creates the situations to which we can choose to react or not react. And it's the internalized voice of the Opponent (the ego) that often makes us choose the path of least resistance. It says, "I'm not to blame for this situation. Others are. I am not to blame for my unhappiness, others are. I am powerless in my own life. I am limited and cannot create my own happiness."

Kabbalists explain that we all have two sides to our nature: one that is negative, reactive, fearful, insecure, and blaming; and one that is capable of anything, is powerful beyond our understanding, is positive, sharing, and takes responsibility. The obstacles that we encounter in life are not really our enemy. As we saw with the king and the harlot, they are the opportunity that the Creator (the king) puts before us in order to give us a chance to become the Creator ourselves. There's not much satisfaction in inheriting a fortune from your rich uncle, especially in comparison to building the fortune on your own against all odds. There's no accomplishment in winning a game that's stacked in your favor.

If you want to be a great tennis player, you may not like it when your opponent returns your best serve, but that doesn't mean you should start playing without someone across the net from you. In fact, the Opponent is a very important concept in Kabbalah. The Opponent exists so we can learn to choose to earn our own happiness.

CREATING THE CIRCUITRY FOR HAPPINESS

If your ultimate joy comes from fulfilling your ultimate responsibility, and your ultimate responsibility is to be completely and permanently joyful, how does knowing all this translate into making it happen?

Your consciousness is the seed for everything that happens to you in this life. Depending on your thoughts, feelings, and actions, you will either access the energy of chaos or the energy of fulfillment. Instead of waiting for some power to come in, solve your problems, and grant your wishes, you need to create a connection with the source of that power. Since that connection to the 99 Percent World has probably happened only sporadically in your life, you need to break out of your habitual ways of living.

Look at it this way: If you were a radio running on batteries, what would happen when the batteries ran down? The radio wouldn't be able to pick up a signal

and broadcast it to whoever was listening. Someone could come along and recharge the old batteries or put in new ones and the radio would play for a while, but then it would run down again. However, if the radio were connected directly into the source of energy, plugged into unlimited wattage, it would be able to transmit its signal at any time. It would be able to share its music with others. It would be happy.

Kabbalah teaches us about the flow of energy and how we can plug into it. It teaches us that the universe operates in two states of existence and through two columns of energy:

Creator	or	Created
Light	or	Vessel
Sharer	or	Receiver
Cause	or	Effect
Powerful	or	Powerless

You're always in one of these two states. The problem is, you may not be aware of which one you're in, or that you have any choice in the matter. The good news is that the choice is always open to you.

Kabbalah is about *circuitry*. It's not a "top-down" system in which God is depicted as an all-powerful father or king. Circuitry means that you are *never* simply an Effect (unless you make the conscious or unconscious choice to be one). You are *never* the pawn of a Divine master. You can *always* improve life at its seed level.

GETTING THE MESSAGE

Imagine you're still feeling a bit sleepy as you get into your car one morning. The next thing you hear is a very unpleasant crunching noise: you've backed right into a car behind you. That will cost you the price of two new bumpers. If asked to explain why this accident happened, would you blame it on the other driver?

If someone were to tell you there was a vital spiritual message about your life concealed in this incident, what would your reaction be?

Suppose you got into a second accident of the same kind only a day later. Would you be more inclined to believe there was something going on beyond the perception of your five senses? What if a similar accident happened every day for a week? Would it just be simple coincidence?

Here's what you need to understand: Everything in your life is exactly as it should be *right now*, based on what you need *at this moment* to move your soul forward toward ultimate happiness.

The car accident described above may have seemed like a random event, but there's a way in which the accident (and all the events of your life) are the manifestation of something much larger. Kabbalah teaches that your soul has passed through the world in many different life spans. In each of these lifetimes, there was a specific aspect of your soul that needed to be corrected before you could move on to the next stage of your spiritual journey. You can ignore the message that is being sent to you, but if you do, the message will continue to be sent until you take positive action to make your correction.

Problems in our lives are really messages that need to be heard and addressed. In the example of the car accident, it may be that an accident of some kind occurred in the past—perhaps even in another lifetime—for which you may have blamed someone else and failed to take responsibility. Now you've been presented with an opportunity to correct that situation. You need to not react to the fender-bender by getting angry and excusing yourself from blame. Instead, use it as an opportunity to move your soul past a sticking point by accepting responsibility.

Whether you are right or wrong in the everyday world is much less important than whether you choose to connect to energy that will move you beyond blame and into happiness.

CHOOSING TO TAKE CHARGE

How do you turn around the circumstances of your life so you're in control, so you're the Creator of your own happiness? No matter what the situation might be, there is always a way. Finding that way is the key to unlocking your destiny of ultimate happiness.

Many people have had an unhappy childhood for one reason or another. Some will use that experience to move forward in their lives, while others will remain stuck in the role of blaming themselves or others (even blaming those who are long gone from their lives).

My mother and teacher, Karen Berg, explained a powerful kabbalistic concept in one of her lectures. In speaking about abusive relationships from the point of view of reincarnation, she said that the reason a person is abused in this lifetime, difficult as it might be to accept, is that they were an abuser in a past life. The cycle of abuser/abused stops when the person's soul, their individual spark of the Light, says, "That's enough! The debt has been paid."

All that may be needed is to switch your thinking. There is always a choice: "I can cry about the abuse I've suffered and thus remain stuck in my suffering, or I can rise above the situation, turn my pain into growth, and become someone who helps do something to remove pain and suffering from the world. I can take the lump of clay I've been handed and sculpt it into something beautiful. I refuse to think of myself as powerless any longer! I can leave this abusive situation. I'm making a decision, a conscious choice: From now on, *I am powerful and in charge of my life!*"

It may sound simplistic, but it works! "I am in charge of my life," is more than just a mantra to repeat over and over again. That consciousness, that awareness, is the switch to activating a spiritual technology that connects you to a source of joy so powerful that it fills every empty space in your life.

God never blames. God makes things happen. The moment you take responsibility for what you do with whatever hand you've been dealt, you become like The Creator. You plug into the 99 Percent World and connect to the Light. Now, by tapping in, you create your own newly carved destiny. Suddenly, people feel a different energy from you. Let's face it, there is a world of difference between the energy of someone who is creative, inspired, willing to take chances and be responsible for the outcomes, and the energy of some- one who always seeks the approval of others, defends themselves, feels they are being "done to," and is afraid to step out of the box lest they get hurt. Who would you rather have a relationship with, work with, play with?

Who would you rather be?

Remember the two columns? As a victim, you are pow- erless, the Created, the Vessel, the Receiver, the Effect. When you take charge of your life, you become power- ful, the Creator, the Light, the Sharer, and the Cause.

THE POWER OF GIVING

One of the Opponent's cleverest tricks begins when we're still in the crib. As infants we're helpless, and when we cry with pain from our empty bellies someone comes along to feed us. Very quickly we learn to manipulate the world around us to first get what we need, and as we get older and more capable, to get what we want. The Opponent sees to it that the lesson we take away from our helpless infancy is that life is about acquiring, about taking or receiving rather than about giving.

The reason this is so brilliant is that the Opponent has succeeded in teaching us that things are exactly the opposite of how they truly are. If you ever read Superman comics as a child you may remember Bizarro World, a place in which things are the opposite of how they are here on Earth: what people say is the opposite of what they mean. The Opponent has us living in Bizarro World because once we've survived infancy, *taking only moves us away from what we really want and need. It only gives us Bread of Shame. Giving is the real source of power in our lives. It makes us the Cause, not merely the Effect. It makes us God.*

Have you ever felt broke, but found it in your heart to come up with a few quarters for that homeless person, or a few dollars to drop into that Salvation Army bucket? If so, do you remember how you felt in that moment? I'm guessing you felt powerful, as you realized that there are people in far greater need than you are, and you're choosing to help them. Power comes from giving. Powerlessness comes from taking.

Blaming works the same way. When you accept full responsibility, you're giving yourself the gift of true power. You're making yourself like the Creator. When you blame, you give that power away. You make some one else the Cause, and yourself the Effect.

THE LAW OF ATTRACTION

According to Kabbalah, the secret of all secrets is the Law of Attraction. According to this universal Law, *Like Attracts Like.* When you are not like God, you create distance between yourself and the 99 Percent World, which results in chaos and darkness. When you let go of being a victim and become the Cause of the circumstances in your life, you are now identical to God—the Cause of all Causes. Like Attracts Like. Again, *Like Attracts Like.* Repeat it to yourself because it happens to be the hidden key to your supreme fulfillment: LIKE ATTRACTS LIKE!

So when you are the Cause, you are *like* God. Why? God is the ultimate Cause and, by acting like God, you achieve closeness and oneness with God. Take a boulder that has been chipped away from a mountain, stick it back into the mountain, and the boulder *becomes* the mountain. They are indistinguishable from one another. The only reason you call it a rock, or a stone, or a boulder is because it has been separated from the mountain from which it originated.

You place yourself back into the mountain we call God when you emulate God, when you are like God. That means accepting responsibility for being the *Cause* of your own chaos. Period. No buts. No arguments. No questions. Full responsibility. No matter what. Now, when you are God, you *can answer your own prayers.* You can do anything. So accepting responsibility is actually the most powerful prayer we can ever hope to make. Profound. Earth-shattering. It's about greed of a kind, because it's about "what's in it for me?" The answer is: *Everything!*

And what do we do when we run off the rails? We pray to an external God. We pray as victims instead of accepting responsibility. We ask an outside force to solve our problems. Or we ask our accountants. Or lawyers. Or friends. And we point the finger of blame at others. Or we point it heavenward. And when the chaos increases, we "pray" harder to God for more help.

See what's wrong with this picture? Now we are doing the exact opposite of true prayer (which is taking responsibility). Thus, all of our so-called prayers are actually driving us farther away from God. Like attracts like. Say it ten times a day. Say it a hundred times. Mind-blowing. Any wonder our prayers go unanswered? When we pray to an external God, we are being an Effect, the opposite of God, so we're creating separation between ourselves and God.

Our prayers are actually creating even more distance between ourselves and the 99 Percent.

What a hoax, what a plan, what brilliant strategy by the Opponent!

And now, he will give you 63 reasons why this isn't true, in an effort to plant doubt in your mind.

THE CREATOR

Where did this feeling of blaming and "victimhood" come from in the first place? It was created to keep us from becoming God. It was created by the Opponent— our self-centered egotistical attitude—to prevent us from unleashing our God-like power to control our world and our lives . . . and our egos!

When most of our time is spent in the land of *I-me-mine*, our minds narrow, our world shrinks. When we have a personal problem, it seems huge, insurmountable. When we become more like God—more like the Creator, the one who shares with others, the Cause and not the Effect—our world expands. Now our problems become manageable—because we are willing to assume full responsibility for them. They don't loom quite so large.

So we have to *earn* the power of God through dedicated effort. We have to *earn* our birthright and destiny, which is to have endless happiness and joy, created by

our own hands. And we develop our creative power in direct proportion to our success at eradicating ego and selfishness. Thus, sharing and ego-restriction are powerful ways to help us evolve the strength to accept responsibility. Selfishness is what prevents us from taking responsibility. The less selfish we are, the easier it is for us to accept responsibility. And when we accept responsibility for our own thoughts, words, and deeds, we unleash the Godly power within us. It's all connected. Thus, sharing, kindness, and resisting reactive behavior are all tools designed to awaken the strength and foresight to be accountable for everything!

So you see what's at stake here? When we accept responsibility, we become God. It's not a matter of morality, it's a purely practical approach: it works!

When we are God, imagine our power. The only weapon the Opponent has is to make us feel like victims. It's a trap. A trick. Deception. And we buy into it. We fall for it every minute of every hour of every day, seven days a week. Imagine what would happen to our life and this

world if everyone stopped for one moment and accepted full responsibility for everything. The chaos would
be over. The doubts implanted by the Opponent would
be gone.

When you become God, everything changes.
Everything. You have just unlocked the power to
achieve boundless fulfillment.

MOVING BEYOND BLAME

Since blame is a well-established habit for most of us, you need to go Beyond Blame ASAP. Blame is not part of being the Cause of your own happiness. As long as blame remains part of your world view, you are cutting yourself off from real joy.

Instead of saying, "Why me?" when something happens, suppose you cut out the "me," and ask, "Why? What's the real reason this situation has come into my life? If I restrict my negative impulse to blame something or someone outside of myself, what positive responses open up to me? How can I use what's happened to become more like the Creator?"

Here's an example of how this system works.

Suppose you really want a lasting relationship, but since you haven't found your soul mate yet, a sexual encounter is sounding pretty good. You can make a conscious decision: "I know this is not a substitute for a loving deep relationship, but I will settle for good sex at this point. If in the end I get hurt, I am not a victim because I walked into this situation with my eyes open." Although this may not have been the smartest decision in the world, at least by not feeling like a victim, you are connecting to some small portion of the Light. Don't misunderstand me. I am not suggesting that having a one-night stand is a good idea. I am merely using this as an example of the choices that we are faced with in life. To really understand the effects of this type of sexual encounter, you can read my book, *The Kabbalah Book of Sex: And Other Mysteries of the Universe.* But for the purpose of this book, let's look at it from the point of view of blame.

The biggest problem with being a victim is the game we play with ourselves. We make silent decisions without really thinking about them, and then we find ourselves in situations where we blame others for hurting us: "Boo-hoo. I slept with him and he broke my heart. Why me?"

If the decision to have sex was made consciously, then you can no longer be the victim: "I wanted to have sex, and I enjoyed it. It was my choice. I take responsibility and I will pay the energetic bill collector and move on."

GUILT

There is a big difference between taking responsibility and blaming yourself—a big, big difference. You may know that no one else is to blame for your problems, but you may decide that it's all your fault. You're to blame. You can't do anything right. You really fouled up this time, and all you can do is wallow in your failure. That's blame turned inward, and it's called *guilt.*

Guilt is not the result of taking responsibility. The Opponent would like us to think we are taking responsibility by feeling badly about what we did, but it's an illusion. In reality, guilt changes nothing. If you beat yourself up mentally, emotionally, or physically, you're just depleting the energy you need to change. Choosing to stay in guilt can lead to depression. You can become paralyzed with guilt, unable to move forward in life.

The way to move out of guilt is the same as moving out of blame: take an action to be like the Creator. The

Creator does not have a need for self-abuse. The Creator merely shares, creates, initiates. The next time you feel guilty about something, take responsibility for what you have done and make a commitment to change. Then take an action of sharing in order to connect to the 99 Percent. Download the energy to give you the power to change. It's as simple as that.

TRY IT!

During the next few days (or even the next few hours) something will probably happen to trigger your "blame response." Unfortunately, you've probably been using that response all your life. It's well engrained, so you'll have to be very conscious in order to respond in a different way.

Even if it seems like you're a totally innocent victim, see what happens if you *accept total responsibility*. See what happens when you realize that every difficulty in your life has been chosen by you, at the deepest level of your soul, so that you can overcome the Opponent and use the challenge to become the Cause of your own happiness. Not even the Creator can coerce you into changing your own destiny. After all, if change came from outside yourself, then you would not be the one who fulfilled your responsibility for creating your own ultimate happiness.

The role of victim can be very seductive. There's a certain pleasure in feeling sorry for yourself, even if you know in your soul that you're only playing a part. Chaos, pain, suffering, and even death are illusions, just as darkness is an illusion made convincing by the absence of light.

So go beyond blame. When you feel like the world is picking on you, ask yourself, "What pleasure am I getting from this feeling? How can I stop chasing that pleasure and exchange it for what I really want?"

When you think that God has forgotten about you, tell yourself this: "I will remind myself of the spiritual truth I know but have forgotten—that God is within me!"

When your life seems too difficult and demanding, say this: "I will find ways to make life easier for others—not out of altruism, but from the ultimate self-interest. It will make my life better!"

When everything is going wrong and there seems to be too much evil in the world, tell yourself, "I bring more good into my life and the lives of those around me."

IT'S OKAY TO FALL DOWN

You don't have to be perfect at being responsible right out of the box. Don't even try. It's OK to fall into feeling like the victim every once in a while. We all do. The difference now is that when you fall into it, you'll *know* who the real enemy is. It's not the person out there you should be blaming. It's your Opponent who is making you feel powerless. So losing one round of the fight is not a problem. The problem is not even knowing or remembering that you are in a fight with the Opponent. When you are in the grips of blame, try to remember you can change the situation. It doesn't matter if you fall down; just pick yourself up, dust yourself off, and remember: it's always your choice.

A KABBALISTIC TALE

Before going on to the personal accounts that make up the balance of this book, let's look for a moment at a much older story that reveals the kabbalistic perspective.

Once, in a small town in Eastern Europe, there was a man named Jacob. His life seemed to be full of problems and pain. For one thing, he and his wife had never been able to conceive a child. They had very little money, every day was filled with nothing but hard work, and there seemed to be no way out.

Finally Jacob went to see the famous kabbalistic teacher known as the Baal Shem Tov, or Master of the Good Name. The teacher listened to Jacob's many problems, and also to the blame that Jacob directed at various people as explanations for those problems. After hearing all this, the Baal Shem Tov gave Jacob some mysterious advice: "Go to a certain town whose name I will give you. Tell the first person you meet there that you have come to see a man named Josef, and ask where this Josef might be found."

Jacob was puzzled by all this, and when the Baal Shem Tov told him the name of the town, he realized that it was very far away. Still, no one ever questioned the great teacher's wisdom, so Jacob departed on the journey.

When he finally arrived at the edge of the town that the Baal Shem Tov had named, the first person he met was a blacksmith who was busy shoeing a horse. "Excuse me," Jacob said, "but I've been sent here to look for a man named Josef. Do you know if there's anyone by that name in this town?"

The blacksmith looked up, hesitated a moment, and then shook his head. "Long ago," he said, "there was someone here named Josef, but he's dead now, and no one here has named their child Josef ever since. He was a really nasty person. You wouldn't have liked him. We're all better off now that he's gone."

After hearing this news, Jacob had no choice but to begin the long trip home. As he did so, he felt worse than ever. He had devoted considerable time and effort to this journey, and he had nothing to show for it. As usual, he looked for someone to blame for the pain and desperation he felt, but there was no one to blame except for the Baal Shem Tov. It felt strange to blame the great teacher, but Jacob could not see his situation in any other way.

Jacob hurried to see the Baal Shem Tov as soon as he returned home and demanded, "Why did you send me on such a long journey to find some man named Josef, who's been dead for so many years? Not only that, but how could this Josef have possibly helped me deal with all the problems in my life? He seems to have been a really awful person."

The Baal Shem Tov replied in a quiet voice, "Even though you didn't get to meet Josef, I think that just hearing about him will help you understand the way things have been going for you. You see, in a past life, you were Josef."

This story touches on kabbalistic teachings about reincarnation, which we mentioned earlier. But even without delving deeply into reincarnation, there is still a powerful message here. Even within a single lifetime, we can be many different people.

Many people are like Jacob. They're unhappy with what's happening to them, and they look outside themselves for something to blame. What they need to learn—and as we've seen it's not an easy lesson—is that even when things seem far beyond our responsibility, we always have the power to change who we are, if only we can recognize that power and use it to improve our lives. To grow beyond blame, and to enjoy the benefits of that growth, accepting responsibility is absolutely essential. Please bear that in mind as you read the stories in the next section. Even more important, bear it in mind as you live your life every day.

Part Three

THE BEYOND
BLAME STORIES

The stories that make up the balance of this book were not dreamed up by professional writers. They are true accounts of people's life experiences, in their own words. As you'll see, not everyone shares the same perspective, as the writers are at different points in their spiritual work, different stages of their process. As you read their stories, ask yourself which ones seem closest to you, not necessarily in what happened, but in the thoughts and the feelings that they communicate.

Then, read back over the first section of this book and try thinking about the stories from a kabbalistic viewpoint. Without judging anyone, be aware of which ones seem to be moving Beyond Blame and toward taking responsibility.

You might consider writing up your own life experience. You can let your thoughts wander across your life until you settle on a specific incident or relationship—one that may have caused you pain in the past and may still cause some pain. You may find that this changes as you write about it. Or maybe nothing will change. Experiment. What do you feel? What have you learned?

If you find that the writing experiment opened your eyes to your own dilemma, you might want to let others see what you've written. You can upload your story anonymously on www.72.com and also read contributions by other writers. You can be sure that no one will interpret or criticize anything you write. The goal is not to evaluate how far anyone has come on their soul's journey, but to show how many different paths that journey can take as we all make the trek to the ultimate happiness that is our true destiny.

You can also keep an ongoing journal, a day-to-day examination of your life, which will help you see more clearly the places you are stuck and the times that you slip into blame and feeling like a victim.

* * *

My parents divorced when I was two years old, and we moved directly from my father's house to my stepfather's. My stepfather was always very possessive of my mom, so he wouldn't let my brother and sister and me come close to my mom. That meant not coming into their bedroom, not touching our mom, and them going on vacation without us. I was first apart from my mom when I was two years old, when they left on their honeymoon for three months. It was so shocking for me. When I think of it, I still feel like crying, and I get this abandoned, unprotected, unsecured feeling.

I had a problem wetting my bed when I was three or four years old. I would wake up in the middle of the night, wet and cold, but I couldn't go to my mom because my stepfather would freak out. So I would try to change my clothes and fix the bed myself, feeling so sad and lonely.

Beginning when I was five years old, my stepfather convinced my mom to send us to camp for a whole month every summer so they could go on vacation without us. Later on, they would go out of the country on vacations with the kids from their marriage, and leave the rest of us at home.

Every time there was a birthday party of a friend, I would always be the last one invited, and every time there was a play or another event at school, nobody would show up to see me. I always felt a little sad for some reason, even though we did have some good moments. My mom would try to make us feel happy and loved when her husband was not around. She would try to defend us as best she knew how, but she was trapped by the need to make this marriage work.

When I was six years old, my real father left the country and didn't come back until I was 22 years old. The only contact we had with him was a birthday card or phone call. My stepfather constantly let us know that my father was not helping financially, and that all the burden for taking care of us was falling on him, though my mom was working very hard also and we would hardly ever see her. She would come home from work around 9 p.m. every night.

So we grew up with this feeling of not deserving much, and also of guilt—because my mom would give us as much as she could behind her husband's back. It must have been to relieve the guilt she was also feeling.

At one point, my stepfather's son decided to move in with us. He had a history of behavior problems at school. We used to have a dog that we all loved so much, and she suddenly started to have all kinds of problems. Finally the vet told my parents that the dog had been abused by someone. She died after a while. I'm sure it was my stepfather's son who did it. When I think of my dog, I still feel the same pain that I felt then.

When I was 18 years old, a friend from out of the country stayed with us for a year. We had a very special connection and started dating. I was completely in love. Then this friend began to socialize with my stepfather's son. After a while, my boyfriend told me that my stepfather's son told him about all sorts of things that supposedly had happened to me. I was shocked and had no idea what he was talking about. He said, "Don't worry, you can tell me everything." But I kept on insisting that I had no idea what he was talking about.

Suddenly I started to remember. Memories had been buried somewhere in my mind, but then I realized that they had really happened. I was so depressed. My first reaction was that nobody should ever know about this abuse—I wanted to hide it, to erase it. I did not want to remember or to admit it happened. All of that is still hard for me, even now.

My boyfriend decided that it was not good for me to hide these memories, so he told my stepfather what happened. My stepfather, who I really tried to avoid, tried to convince me that things happen sometimes, and that the way to deal with it was to forgive and understand. He just wanted to brush it off so it wouldn't bring more complications to his marriage, I guess, and I had a strong desire to pretend it never happened. It made me feel even more undefended when people tried to excuse it with explanations.

Today, even as a grown woman, I feel like blaming my mom for leaving me unprotected and abandoned at that time. I've gotten a little better lately using the tools I have recently learned in Kabbalah, and I am starting to learn how to resist behaviors and beliefs that make me feel powerless, and to allow myself to feel I am worthy of good things, like knowing that someone can be there for me—that I can count on someone other than myself.

* * *

As a young boy I was fascinated by the fact that my father and other members of my family were combat war veterans. It seemed particularly strange because they were all very gentle people who mainly liked to work, play cards, and watch sports events. There was not much fighting in my family, no yelling, and no drinking.

My father was born into real poverty and had spent much of his childhood in an orphanage, which he left at age fourteen to begin working. He became very successful, and I believe he associated fighting and other domestic "drama" with a world he had worked very hard to leave behind. But as it turned out, even without fighting there was plenty of drama in our home.

I am not sure when my mother was first diagnosed with cancer, but by the time I was six years old she was suffering from pain that was terrible to see. She died when I was eight. I was an only child, and I guess my father didn't feel he could handle raising me by myself. I think it might have been easier for him—and certainly for me—if there had been older brothers or sisters to help raise me, but that was not the way it was. We never really talked about this. For all his good intentions, my father was not comfortable exploring difficult emotions. Instead, he liked to take quick action to deal with problems.

Soon he hired a live-in nanny to be responsible for me on a day-to-day basis. I quickly smelled trouble. I was very loyal to my mom, and from the first I was horrified by the possibility that my father might become involved with this new woman in our home. For his part, I think that's exactly what my father intended—not because he wanted a lot of romance in his life, but because he felt he needed to remarry and leave me with someone in case he died too. He was considerably older than my mom, and I think he knew he was not going to "live forever."

I was almost ten years old, and I did everything I could to make life miserable for the new nanny—let's call her C. She was actually a very intelligent, attractive, and responsible woman in her late 30s, but I saw her as a symbol of betrayal. And my worst fears came true. Late one night, as I sneaked around the apartment, I caught them embracing. Again, my father didn't know how to talk to me about what was going on. It wasn't the kind of thing they taught in the orphanage. In any case, one day he took me aside and handed me a marriage license. At first I thought it was a joke, something that he'd gotten out of a vending machine. But then I saw that he and C. had really married. He said something about wanting me to have a mom again, but I was horrified.

For several years, I continued to have a difficult relationship with C. I never really accepted her as part of the family, and she never really felt she had been accepted.

When I was fifteen, my father was diagnosed with lung cancer. This was really a very bad and scary time, which had many negative repercussions. For one thing, it made me a complete cancer hypochondriac—a condition that secretly tortured me for many years. My father died about a year after his diagnosis, when I was sixteen.

Now it was just C. and me. Again, it might have been less intense if there had been some siblings, but there were none. I had developed a pretty formidable teenage attitude that probably intimidated C. It was hard for her to deal with my refusal to accept her as an authority figure. When I was seventeen, I went away to an Ivy League college. Over the next five years, I flunked out, hitchhiked around Mexico, got drafted, got kicked out of the military for taking drugs, wound up in the psychiatric ward of a hospital, started intensive psychotherapy, returned to the same college, and eventually graduated. Within a few months of leaving school I got married.

Now, flash forward about fifteen years. Many things had changed in the past decade and a half, and I had grown up to some extent. My relationship with C. had certainly improved. She had never remarried after my father's death, but she had an extended family and a group of friends who kept her from feeling isolated. She became ill, and over the next six months she completely deteriorated mentally and physically: Finally she reached a point where she had had enough; she told her doctors that she wanted to stop any further medication or treatment, and she died about two weeks after that.

I was with C. most of the time during her final illness, and after she died one of the things I had to take care of was cleaning everything out of her apartment. No one enjoys doing something like that, and I certainly didn't enjoy it. C. had sometimes worked as a book-keeper after my father died, and she was always very careful about money. In one of her closets I found boxes of canceled checks going back more than twenty years. For some reason, looking at all those checks really affected me. I saw all the expenses, big and small, that had gone into raising a stepchild by herself. The grocery bills, the school charges, the payments to the psychiatrist when I was causing problems.

Also in that closet I found a bunch of letters I had written to C. during my first year in college, when I was seventeen. When I first read the letters, I thought they must have been part of some extended practical joke I was playing on C. I couldn't have been writing this seriously! I was stunned by what a totally selfish, whining twit the writer of these letters seemed to be. I couldn't identify with that person. I certainly couldn't believe it was me, but it was. I had seen myself completely as a victim of the world's injustice. I was really shocked by it. True, there had been things in my life—like the death of my parents—that might explain this. But explaining is different from justifying. The way I had expressed myself to C. seemed totally out of line.

On the other hand, I was encouraged by the fact that I must have definitely changed since then. I wasn't conscious of changing, because I had never been aware of what I had been like. But I certainly was no longer that person, thank God.

Now I am the parent of a girl who is just turning thirteen. Sometimes she says and does things that shock me. I feel like I'm trying as hard as I can for her every day, but she still likes to see herself as a victim. This gives me three valuable opportunities. First, I can remember the way I was when I was at her point in life and, in fact, even when I was older. Second, I can resist the impulse to see myself as a victim right now, to feel sorry for myself, to feel unappreciated, to feel wronged, and so on and so forth. And lastly I can work with my daughter to see that we both become givers rather than takers. Giving to others turns out to be a great way to give ourselves that powerful, warm feeling of knowing you've made a difference in someone else's life. These are ideas that Kabbalah has helped to clarify for me. For more than seven years now, I have studied Kabbalah every day, and it's difficult for me to see how I would understand my life without the things I've learned.

* * *

As a child, I had a very difficult time with my father and I grew up feeling victimized by him. There were many painful incidents in my childhood, and also in my first marriage—one negative situation after another. When I began to study Kabbalah, I explained or justified all this by connecting it to reincarnation. The problems must have originated from something in a past life. But deep inside I still felt like a victim. I felt like someone had done me wrong, and that someone was my father. How could he have done that to me? He was supposed to love me. He was supposed to be there for me.

It all came to a head about eight years ago, when my father took me to court. He accused me of being an unfit mother and tried to take my children away from me. I thought, "How can a father do something like that? How can a father do that to his daughter? How can he do it to his grandchildren?" In court it was really awful as I faced all his malicious fabrications.

Throughout all of that, I was studying Kabbalah and using the tools of Kabbalah. In court, I scanned *The Zohar*. I felt there was a lesson for me to learn in what was happening, and that it was related to something from a past life. But inside I was still thinking, "How can a father do something like this?"

Finally all the charges against me were dismissed and the court case ended. Grandfathers can't take kids away. After a lot of ugliness, it was done. But my father and I didn't speak for the next five years.

Then my mother came to visit and told me an interesting story. My mother and my father are divorced, but his second wife told my mom about something that had happened 25 years ago. When my father married his second wife, they made an appointment with an in vitro specialist to try to have a child. It took months to get the appointment, but when they finally walked into the office my father said, "You know, I'm not interested in doing this"—and he walked out. His second wife never could figure out why he did that.

Listening to this, my mind went back 25 years. I was nineteen. My father's new wife seemed wonderful, in all the ways that I was not. She had beautiful daughters, and I didn't feel like a beautiful daughter. I was very threatened by his new life and what it meant for me. My parents had divorced when I was seven, and except for all the difficult times I'd had with my father, there had not been much else between us. I began working in his company right before he remarried, and at last I felt we had started to have a real relationship, that he was finally turning into a normal father. But then he got married and brought in these two new daughters. So what did that mean for me? What was going to happen to me? It was all about me.

Then I remembered how he had sat me down in his office and said, "So what would you think if Laura and I had a child?" And I said, "Why? Why do you want to have a child? I'm going to get married soon, and I'll have a child. What will happen then? Your child will play with your grandchild?"

Thinking about this 25 years later, knowing everything I have learned in these intervening years, I am so ashamed and disturbed by how selfish and self-centered I was. I realized how important it would have been for him to have a child. Even apart from the spiritual side, it would have been really nice for him to perhaps have a son. I also realized that, in some way, by walking out of the doctor's office, he was trying to make it up to me for his being such a difficult father. In his mind, this was a way of being good to me. He wanted to show me that he had changed. But I really didn't want to see that he had changed. I was *comfortable* being a victim, so in my mind I kept him in the box marked "awful person" until eventually it led to the court case.

When the court case was happening, I went to a kabbalistic astrologer. She told me, "One of the reasons your father's doing this is that he feels you owe him, and that maybe somewhere or in some way your children are his children." At the time, I didn't understand what she meant except in terms of reincarnation and past lives. But now I realize that, to him, my children represented the kids he might have had. And I was really struck by how so many destinies can be changed by one stupid, ugly thing that a nineteen-year-old can say. We don't realize the power of our words and the damage and hurt we can cause.

After not having spoken to him in the five years since the court case, I called him the next day. I said, "Dad, I'm really sorry. I know that I was a difficult daughter, and that I judged you harshly. You did the best you could, you tried to make it up to me, and I never let you." He said, "You know, I can't forgive you, because some things are too late to fix." I knew he meant the conversation about having a child with his second wife.

He also knew that I knew. I said to him, "I understand, but I just want you to know that I'm really sorry."

Many months passed and we still did not talk. I felt such pain at how I'd taken away the opportunity he could have had in his life. I realized that we're never victims. We are the Creators of everything that happens, and referring it to a past lifetime is a cop-out. It's all right here in this lifetime. Everything we do, everything we say, and everything we think. We have no idea how powerful those things are. And again, I felt such pain.

But that was not the end. A few weeks later, I had a phone call from one of my friends in Toronto. She said, "You know, a funny thing happened. I ran into your dad and his wife in a restaurant, and his wife told me that after 25 years your dad decided to go back to that In vitro doctor." I was completely shocked! I thought, "For 25 years he must have put it completely out of his mind. Then I tell him I'm sorry, and he doesn't forgive me, but now he wants to go back to the doctor!"

Nothing came of that in terms of my dad having a child. But our relationship grew and became much better and more real than it ever was before—without me being a victim and without him having to be the abuser. It must have been such a relief for him. Now he also has a relationship with my kids. Life changed for the better after that for all of us.

* * *

I was born into a family that was broken into pieces. My older brothers and sisters were one part of the family— three from my mom's first marriage, and three from my dad's first marriage—although only one of them lived with us. Then there were me and my little brother, who was two years younger. So there were "my kids," "your kids," and "our kids"—lots of fragments.

Another fragmentation was between my parents themselves. They fought a lot and usually involved me in it. I remember thinking, when I was seven years old, "Why can't I be normal like other kids in my school?" From a very young age I saw myself as a victim who was forced to take sides. My dad would encourage me to be close to his son, who lived with us. I thought his son was weird, but I felt sorry for him and for my dad. Getting closer to his son was a way for me to gain my dad's approval. Also, it seemed like my father did not want me to be close to my mom's kids. Of course, this created tension between me and my mom.

A good example of this took place when I was nine years old. After a lot of pressure from my dad, I had agreed to go out with his son for ice cream. When I got back home, my mom didn't speak to me. Later that day she said, "I don't care what you do, because I have other kids who really love me." So I grew up with the belief that being close to one person means getting further away from someone else.

I believed I was the only one who cared about both of them. It seemed to me the rest of the kids were either mom's kids or dad's kids. My little brother never got involved, and, as he told me recently, he wasn't even aware of these things. It was like he was in a different universe. This also created further anger and victim feelings inside me, like, "How come he doesn't get involved and he leaves me alone with everything?"

I always felt I owed the other kids something. Often I rejected any attempt at affection by my father. I felt ashamed that he wouldn't treat the other kids as well, so they might feel badly and blame me. I had a constant sense of "not deserving," or "I shouldn't have this or that." I felt that no matter how hard I tried to make people happy, eventually someone made me feel I was not doing it right. That led me to reject love, to reject things my parents wanted to give me, and to feel guilty if I was given anything.

Once, when I was twelve and my parents were having a really loud fight, my mom said something like, "If you want, they can leave the house." This was referring to my siblings. I heard it and they did too. So I ran to them and cried, "Please, never leave!" My older sister was crying. In that moment I felt like I wanted to disappear from the world. I loved my mom, my dad, my brothers and sisters, but there was no way for me to be close to all of them. I always had to choose. Also, I felt everyone's pain and the impossibility of fixing things.

I was a total victim, and I really didn't see any way out. My older brothers and sisters were nasty to me sometimes, but I knew they didn't mean it. Growing up, I couldn't get rid of this feeling of needing to choose. It could be between mom and dad, brother and sister, girlfriends, boyfriends—always feeling that getting closer to someone meant getting further away from someone else.

Actually I just realized this very recently: I always find myself in situations where I need to choose, like when I need to get distance from one person in order to save a relationship with somebody else. Even today, I don't really know how to deal with this. I end up feeling used and sad, and closing myself up to everyone. I've just started studying Kabbalah, and I'm beginning to see how my past experiences and my ego keep me seeing people and social situations as something I need to control. I'm slowly learning to stop seeing myself as someone who needs something from other people, and to start seeing myself as someone who has an amazing amount to give.

* * *

When I was told that I had cancer, two thoughts came into my mind. Why me, and why now? I had studied Kabbalah for seven years, I was using the tools of Kabbalah—how could cancer be happening to me? I was afraid. In the first moments, I was really in shock. And I also felt guilt. If I had been studying for so long, and using the tools, and even teaching Kabbalah, if I could still get cancer, something must be very wrong with me. I absolutely didn't know what to do.

I came to The Centre and called my teacher. I said, "I have cancer." She couldn't believe it: "No, it can't be. It has to be a mistake." But it wasn't a mistake. Cancer was what the doctor said. Still, after talking to my teacher, I felt calmer. I told myself, "Okay, if I need to go through this process, I will do it with the help of the Light and the Rav and Karen and everything in Kabbalah. I have to do it. I have to do the best I can."

I was strong. There were times when I felt weak and I had fears, but mostly I was really strong. I had certainty. It's true that when I started going to doctors and doing my tests, deciding what I was going to do—chemotherapy, yes or no—I went into feeling like a victim and I couldn't fight it. But most of the time I was doing my spiritual work and I was strong.

I went through a mastectomy—they removed a breast on one side—and that was very hard. Then I had to decide about chemotherapy. I thought, "I'm going to do it, but not because I think this will save my life. I'll do it because this is the process I need to live. If it happened to me, it's because there is something in this for me to work on and to learn from. It's something I have to do, so I'll do it. I don't care if it's difficult, and I'm not going to worry about what happens later."

When I started chemotherapy, I realized there were two frameworks for understanding what was happening. One was spiritual: it's happening because I need to learn something, I need to change something. I didn't know what I was supposed to change, but I was sure this must be true, because this is what Kabbalah teaches. But there was also the physical framework of what was happening, and on a physical level I was sick. I had cancer, and because of that I had to do many things that I didn't want to do.

The chemotherapy wasn't easy, but, again, I was strong and I was doing my spiritual work as much as I could. Then the doctor called me one day and asked me to come to the hospital immediately. When I got there, he said, "I'm very sorry to tell you, but we found something else. You have tumors in the liver, and it's not good. I'm sorry."

This was very hard. I didn't say anything. I wanted to hide. I was in shock. It was really, really scary. It was like going down into a hole, a dark hole of fear and self-pity and guilt and every terrible feeling a human being can have. I said to myself, "I'm trying as hard as I can. I'm doing what I'm supposed to be doing. And now I have tumors again, in the liver, so I'm not going to make it?"

I was going to die, and I didn't want to die. I really didn't want to die. I was crying and crying and crying, and I felt so hopeless and helpless. I felt completely like a victim. And then in the middle of all this pain and fear, I heard a voice inside that said, "Why do you forget that I am with you all the time? Why?" And suddenly I stopped being afraid. I remembered the Light, and in that moment I felt myself starting to change.

I actually started to speak to the Light. I said, "I don't know what is happening, and I don't understand why it's happening. But I want to ask you to help me. I don't want to die—not because I'm afraid, but because I did not finish what I'm here for. So please help me to stay in this life. Help me to overcome all this. By myself, I can't do it. I'm doing everything I can; I'm going to make maximum effort to overcome this and to do what's necessary to stay in life, because this is what I want. If I have to die, help me, and if I can still be here, help me also."

In that moment, I felt like the Light was really inside me. I was very calm, and suddenly I was also strong again. I felt like I was part of life again. I went back to The Kabbalah Centre and my friend Ruthie was waiting for me. She has her own story—her father had cancer—and my situation was very hard for her. But she was so strong for me. She asked me what happened when I got called to the hospital, and I was very calm and said, "Well, they found tumors in the liver." I could see that for one moment she was shocked, but then she said, "It's okay, it's all right. If this is what you need to go through, it's okay." And I thought, "Yes, I'm ready. I'm going to do everything I can, but I'm ready for whatever comes."

And that was it. I was finished with thinking. "Why me?" and "I'm so bad." I was finished with the focus needing to be on me. I was going to do my job. I was going to be busy with everything that needed to be done, and that's what I did.

I went for more tests and more examinations. Then, I don't remember if it was one or two weeks later, the doctor called me. When I went to see him I was ready for anything, but there he was with a big smile on his face. He said, "You know what? It's very weird, but now we don't see anything. I honestly don't understand it, because we don't make those kinds of mistakes. But we aren't seeing the tumors we saw before." He actually seemed kind of upset about it. I said, "Doctor, are you happy that you don't see anything now, or do you want to see something?" Then he said, "No, no, of course I'm happy for you! I am very happy for you!"

What did I learn from this whole process? I learned that everything we are going through, no matter what, is really for the best, and when we go through it with this consciousness, everything will be all right. When something happens, we just have to trust the Light, and put ourselves in the hands of the Light. When we want something very badly, we can be fighting so hard that we can't see any farther than the tip of our nose. We don't see what is good for us, or what is best for us. So we have to look outside ourselves and put our attention on others. We can't be preoccupied with our pain and our fears. We have to put ourselves in the hands of the Light, and just do our work.

* * *

My childhood was not an easy one. My mother was sexually abused as a child and tortured on one occasion in Morocco. I am the only one she ever told about this, and when she shared it with me, everything about her suddenly made sense. When I was growing up, she was unable to touch me, hug me, and kiss me. Instead, she was violent and abusive. I was desperate for the love that I knew she felt but couldn't show. I cried myself to sleep every night, wishing for her love. Instead she would put me down and embarrass me in front of other people.

My father was a gambler. As a result, there was very little money in the bank. We lived in a government housing project. My parents had a terrible relationship. I never saw any love between them. My father slept a lot—a sweet man, but very passive. My mother criticized everything he did. She made it clear that he was incompetent. She used to tell me that he hit her, but I never saw this until once when she provoked him. I was ten years old, and my father blamed me, because I had mentioned that my best friend's parents had bought a new house. That set my mother off. My father could not afford to buy a house because he had gambled his money away. He was useless in her eyes. I felt sorry for my father: I knew this hurt him. Then he shouted that it was all my fault, and hit my mother. I was screaming and terrified. For years after that, I was full of guilt and blamed myself for their unhappy marriage

Then my father became very religious, and was very strict with me. My mother also kept me on a tight leash. I was very lonely. I had no one to play with; my brothers were much older than me. Everything was monitored, from where I went to who called me to what I wore. Being religious made no sense, and I hated it. I asked my father, "When can I be free?" He said, "When you are 18 you can do what you like!" Those words were like a beautiful song to me.

By the time I was 16, I was a nervous wreck—shy, introverted, and very angry. I felt insecure even walking past a group of strangers on the street. I caused fights with my friends because I did not know how to communicate that I was in pain and needed help. At home, I was the victim. I felt everyone owed me. I counted the minutes until I turned 18. I worked every Sunday and saved every penny to buy an airplane ticket.

When I was finally ready to leave, my mother said, "How can you do this to me?" I replied, "I'm just doing the same thing you did to your mother. You were the same age as me."

I felt that my parents had created the perfect victim, but I had actually created it myself. I moved to France, but nothing changed. I was still in victim mode, creating dramas, introverted, insecure, depressive. One day, in pouring rain, I was standing on a street corner waiting for the light to turn green. Then I saw a green man coming toward me—a surgeon in his green hospital uniform! I had been hit by a bus! That still makes me laugh: to this day, I have no recollection of what happened.

The doctor said it was a miracle I was alive. This was a turning point in my life. Although I had been hit by a bus, I didn't see myself as a victim. Something inside me changed when I was unconscious for forty-five minutes. I still had fears and insecurities, I was still fighting against victim consciousness, but the depressed teenager began to disappear.

Skipping ahead, I was in a relationship for more than a year. I met Bill when I was finishing my first year of college. Some difficult things had been happening, and I was looking for someone to save me when I met Bill at a night club through a narcissistic jerk with whom I'd been having sex for a week or two. The attraction to Bill was instant and insane. He knew exactly what to say and do to make me addicted to him—and *addicted* is the correct word.

We slept together that night and within a week we were living together, along with five male roommates in a two-bedroom apartment in New York. All the room-mates were mean to me, usually with Bill's knowledge and approval. Bill liked being mean to me also. He lit-erally loved making me cry, and would always say something he knew would hurt me. Then he'd tell me how beautiful I was when I cried. I can't believe I put up with this, but I thought it was what I deserved, that this was all I could expect from life.

About four months into our relationship, I got pregnant, and we decided I would have an abortion. Hours after the surgery, Bill was yelling at me for killing his baby. I was devastated. I immediately went on the pill, with dire consequences. I almost bled to death from it and ended up in the hospital having blood transfusions.

In the emergency room, the doctor asked Bill to leave the room so he could examine me. Afterwards, Bill freaked out because he thought the doctor just wanted to see me naked.

Before going to the hospital, I had made my first attempt to leave Bill. In response, he threatened to tell my mother about the abortion, so I went back to him. A few months later I got the nerve to try again, and this time he threatened to kill himself. I took him back. Then I somehow got the courage to go on an exchange program to Germany. While there, I decided to leave him, no matter what. I haven't talked to him since.

I have not let anyone else be that mean to me, but most of my friends and boyfriends have been pretty awful. They'd manipulate me, lie, make me feel "less than" in some way or other. When this happened, I'd feel confused, overwhelmed, and distrustful of myself: "I must deserve this. I must have done something wrong." I always have a hard time believing in myself and standing up for myself. I expect people to turn on me at any time. I expect them to take advantage of my weaknesses and my good nature. Now that I'm starting to learn about Kabbalah, I'm definitely bringing better people into my life, and the distrust is less, but it's still there.

* * *

Five years ago I was raped in a pub in London. My victim state began just a few hours later when I went home, took a hot shower, threw up what little I tried to eat, and then passed out on the sofa. When I came to, I crawled up the stairs, climbed into bed, and tried to take comfort in the fetal position. My friend Julia came to visit. As we talked, I tried to make sense of the stabbing pain in my womb area, and I told her the following story about what had happened that day.

Visiting in London for a weekend, I had found an old friend's phone number and wondered how he was doing. Actually, I needed to return a book he had loaned me, and also collect $20 he had borrowed. So I called him, and we met at a busy pub in London Piccadilly.

The conversation was pleasant. He didn't seem disturbed that I was dating someone in Holland. I understood this to mean that he was over his interest in me, and I told him I was glad that we could just be friends. But I was also frustrated that he hadn't yet mentioned the $20 he owed me, so I decided to stay for another drink. Then I went to the restroom. A moment later I heard someone enter, and the door slammed shut. There was loud banging on the cubicle I was in, and a man's voice shouting, "Hurry up! Open this door!" When I recognized the voice, I panicked. "What are you doing here?! You must be crazy!" And for some reason I naively added, "This is the ladies' room. I'm sure if you need the toilet you can go next door."

But he kept banging on the door and shouting, so in an attempt to quiet him, I unlocked the door to the cubicle with one hand, while trying to fasten the top button on my pants with the other. In a flash he was pushing the door open and squeezing his large body inside the cubicle. I resisted, and he shoved me backward. I tried to get past him, but he was completely blocking the way, and then he locked the door of the cubicle.

My first question—"What are you doing here!?"—was soon answered as he forced his mouth against mine. As my head hit the wall behind me, I realized there was nowhere to go. I tried to shake my head from side to side, but with each turn his mouth just pressed harder. He was forcing his body against me, and I knew he had no intention of letting me go. My only thought was, "How am I going to get out of here?" I reached for the door and I did manage to unlock it, but he immediately slammed it shut and became even rougher than before, ripping my pants down as I struggled to keep his hands off my chest.

At that moment, it felt like I was no longer there. Totally at peace, I looked down from above, happy to be out of this as I watched it happening to someone else.

It must have been only a few minutes, but time seemed to stop. Then he was backing away, and I was standing there on my wobbly legs. I pulled my pants up from my ankles and said nothing as he opened the door and left the cubicle. I followed. He was trying to talk to me, but I couldn't hear him. I was repeating "What just happened? What just happened?" His voice seemed to be off in the distance although he was right next to me. He said, "I thought you wanted it." Shaking my head gently back and forth, I whispered, "No, no! I didn't want this! I told you no!"

As I described this to Julia, she snapped me back into reality: "This is rape! You said no! You have to go to the police! He raped you!"

But it couldn't be that. It couldn't happen to me. Not that!

I had a sleepless night because of the pain. Nothing helped. It was like someone had tied my ovaries in a terrible knot. My insides burned until I couldn't take it anymore. At eight in the morning, Julia agreed to come with me to the hospital. As I started to explain to the emergency room doctor the cause of my symptoms, she gently refused to continue the examination and advised me that I needed to see a police doctor.

Why me? For years afterward, I begged for an answer to that question. Why did he do this to me? I said "no" and he kept pushing himself on me. I was a victim. How could I see myself as anything else?

The fears started. Fear of having male friends. Fear of blond-haired men. Fear of going out in public, of going into a pub, of going to the bathroom in a pub, of going to Piccadilly London. Fear of getting close to a guy, of physical contact with a male, or even of a simple conversation that could possibly be construed to mean something more. I battled with each of these fears and faced them head-on, one by one. I met a guy I saw as my savior, and he wouldn't let me talk about it for a year.

Exactly a year later, my savior disappeared and it all came back, just as if it were happening for a second time. The wound was exposed again, and this time it took longer to heal. Why did it take longer? It was because something very important needed to happen. I had to recognize that I was not a victim. I had to completely let it go and forgive. I had to use the strength of the Light inside me to detach from the pain and the anger. I had to inject forgiveness for him (which was the hardest part) and also for myself. I had to move on with happiness—with pure Light and with joy.

I must know that I am the Creator of my own life! I am the Cause of my own thoughts and actions. The events of my life are the Effect of that Cause.

But inside, I do hold the memory of the pain. It helps me when I can't feel the pain of another person. I feel my pain and I cry again. I don't want to close the door to my feelings too completely. I have the feeling that I need to find a way to own what happened, to take responsibility for all of it without getting down on myself. Every day I work on finding the right combination for the lock, and the right balance.

* * *

My parents divorced when I was 14. When my dad moved out, I had a lot of insecurity. I wanted him to love me, but I didn't feel his love. Like many wealthy men, my father always thought that people were after his wealth—and with respect to me, that actually was the case. I measured how much he loved me by how much money he gave me. I thought, "He has so much money, and I'm his daughter, so I should get whatever I want." We fought constantly, mostly over things I wanted that he would not give me. He said I had to earn them. But he would give his girlfriend (later his wife) all kinds of things. I felt this was very unfair of him. When he bought her a Mercedes, I said, "What did she do to earn that?"

My parents thought it would be a good idea for me to see a therapist, the first of many, so I could work out my anger issues. I would always make my dad pay the bill because it was his fault that I had to see a therapist in the first place, and therapy was one of the only things I could get him to pay for. Meanwhile, I would talk to these therapists about my father, dissecting our relationship, and blaming him for all my problems. The therapists and I would plot how to manipulate my father and change him into the dad I wanted him to be. I would switch therapists if I felt that he or she couldn't attach blame for whatever problem I was having to my father.

I felt it was his fault that I had problems with men. My insecurity issues were due to him pushing me too much. Nothing I did was ever good enough for him. He pushed me to apply to Harvard Business School—where he, my grandfather, and my great-grandfather had studied—even though I wasn't ready to go. Then, when I wasn't accepted, that was his fault too because he didn't help me enough with my application. Naturally, it was his fault I was working in a career I hated.

After a few weeks of studying Kabbalah, I realized that the problem wasn't really my father. The problem was me. My dad was never the bad father I made him out to be. I was a horrible daughter. I called my father one day and said, "Dad, I used to blame you for not having a good relationship with me. But it was my fault we didn't

have a good relationship, not yours. Instead of appreci-
ating you, I criticized you. I was looking at all your
faults, instead of seeing the good in you. I'm sorry."

I was going through a break-up around this time; I was
leaving the boyfriend I had lived with for three years. I
wasn't paying rent and wasn't making money, which
made breaking up difficult. I called my father, and he
told me if I wanted to leave my boyfriend, he would get
me a place to live. In the past, my dad never gave me
anything. If I wanted something, I had to work for it.
But now my dad bought me an apartment, a condo in
a doorman building in Manhattan. I could not believe it.

I ran to my teacher and said, "Can you believe how
much my father has changed?" My teacher was very
wise. He replied, "Your dad hasn't changed. You've
changed. Your dad was always like this. It's only
because you're different now that he feels he can share
with you."

Recently my father came to visit me in New York. He admitted that there was a time when he didn't like to be with me. Now he's so happy with the change in me. He takes me shopping, we go on trips together, and we both truly enjoy our time together. I have no more agenda about his money. The truth is, that's never what I wanted in the first place. I only wanted his love, and now I have it; I got it by giving my own.

* * *

TACKLING BLAME WITH THE 72 NAMES OF GOD

Now that you've read the stories and pondered them from the point of view of Kabbalah, you may be wondering what is the most effective way to get on with your own work of getting beyond blame. Well, the very best tool of Kabbalah that I know is The 72 Names of God.

These are no ordinary "names." The 72 Names of God are not actual words, but combinations of three Aramaic letters that connect you to an infinite spiritual current that operates at the DNA level of the soul. The Names help you to unleash your own God-like powers and attain control over your physical reality. It is the very same spiritual technology that Moses used to part the Red Sea.

Each of the three letters in a Name has a particular function. The first is a positive charge, the second a negative charge, and the third a grounding wire, forming a circuit of energy that is transmitted directly to your soul. The sacred sequences of letters that comprise the Names are activated visually. The flow of energy is transferred directly to you when your eyes behold the shapes of the Names. You don't even have to be able to read Aramaic.

If you would like to learn more about this ancient kabbalistic tool, consider reading my book, *The 72 Names of God*. For the purposes of this book—helping you to go Beyond Blame—there are three Names that i openheartedly recommend:

The first is **ייל** Letting Go. It helps us release our past pain and suffering and be willing to welcome happiness into our lives.

The second Name is **מנק** Accountability, which works with the questions we have been discussing: "Why me? Why now? What did I do to deserve this?" It helps us leave victim consciousness behind, stop our reactive behavior, and regain control over our lives.

The third name is מלה Sharing the Flame, which reveals the secret of light and darkness in the everyday world: a single candle can extinguish the darkness. When we share the Light, we lessen our own selfish nature and connect to the 99 percent realm, the infinite source of true happiness and fulfillment. Therefore, this Name has the power to bring us endless joy.

In order to make these Names work for you, it's important to have certainty in their power, understand the particular influence radiating from each Name, and follow through by activating their power with action. It is the follow-through action of going beyond blame that you have been reading about here.

As these three particular Names suggest, we have to have the courage to Let Go of the past, hold ourselves Accountable for our own happiness, and Share the Light to eradicate the darkness. This is the practical wonder of Kabbalah: it doesn't require years of silent contemplation on a mountaintop, and it works in the here and now of our day-to-day lives.

I know, it's not easy, but you're not alone. If you want the advice and help of a qualified teacher of Kabbalah, contact one of our Centres through our website, www.kabbalah.com. If you're not physically near a Centre, the website offers ways to work with a teacher online.

It's your life. Accomplish your true destiny by accepting responsibility for it. May you be happy and totally fulfilled.

If you were inspired by this book in any way and would like to know how you can continue to enrich your life through the power of Kabbalah, here is what you can do next: Read the book *The Power of Kabbalah* or listen to the *Power of Kabbalah* audio tapes.

The Power of Kabbalah

Imagine your life filled with unending joy, purpose, and contentment. Imagine your days infused with pure insight and energy. This is *The Power of Kabbalah*. It is the path from the momentary pleasure that most of us settle for, to the lasting fulfillment that is yours to claim. Your deepest desires are waiting to be realized. But they are not limited to the temporary rush from closing a business deal, the short-term high from drugs, or a passionate sexual relationship that lasts only a few short months.

Wouldn't you like to experience a lasting sense of wholeness and peace that is unshakable, no matter what may be happening around you? Complete fulfillment is the promise of Kabbalah. Within these pages, you will learn how to look at and navigate through life in a whole new way. You will understand your purpose and how to receive the abundant gifts waiting for you. By making a critical transformation from a reactive to a proactive being, you will increase your creative energy, get control of your life, and enjoy new spiritual levels of existence. Kabbalah's ancient teaching is rooted in the perfect union of the physical and spiritual laws already at work in your life. Get ready to experience this exciting realm of awareness, meaning, and joy.

The wonder and wisdom of Kabbalah has influenced the world's leading spiritual, philosophical, religious, and scientific minds. Until today, however, it was hidden away in ancient texts, available only to scholars who knew where to look. Now after many centuries, *The Power of Kabbalah* resides right here in this one remarkable book. Here, at long last is the complete and simple path—actions you

can take right now to create the life you desire and
deserve.

The Power of Kabbalah Audio Tapes

The Power of Kabbalah is nothing less than a user's guide
to the universe. Move beyond where you are right now to
where you truly want to be—emotionally, spiritually, cre-
atively. This exciting tape series brings you the ancient,
authentic teaching of Kabbalah in a powerful, practical
audio format.

You can order these products from our Web site or by calling Student Support.

Student Support: Trained instructors are available 18 hours a day. These dedicated people are willing to answer any and all questions about Kabbalah and help guide you along in your effort to learn more. Just call **1-800-kabbalah**.

MORE FROM NATIONAL BEST-SELLING AUTHOR YEHUDA BERG

The Kabbalah Book of Sex: & Other Mysteries of the Universe

The world is full of sex manuals instructing the reader on the ins and outs of great sex, but these tend to focus on only one aspect, the physical mechanics. According to Kabbalah, the key to fulfilling sex lies in self-awareness, not simply technique. Sex, according to Kabbalah, is the most powerful way to experience the Light of the Creator. It is also one of the most powerful ways to transform the world.

So why doesn't great sex happen all the time in our relationships? Why has the sexual act been so deeply linked to guilt, shame, and abuse? Why do long-term couples lose the spark and get bored with sex? *The Kabbalah Book of Sex* provides a solid foundation for understanding the origins of sex and its purpose, as well as practical kabbalistic tools to ignite your sex life. This ground-breaking guide teaches how to access higher levels of connection—to ourselves, our partners, and to spirit—and achieve unending passion, profound pleasure, and true fulfillment.

The 72 Names of God: Technology for the Soul™

The story of Moses and the Red Sea is well known to almost everyone; it's even been an Academy Award–winning film. What is not known, according to the internationally prominent author Yehuda Berg, is that a state-of-the-art technology is encoded and concealed within that biblical story. This technology is called The 72 Names of God, and it is the key—your key—to ridding yourself of depression, stress, creative stagnation, anger, illness, and other physical and emotional problems. In fact, The 72 Names of God is the oldest, most powerful tool known to mankind—far more powerful than any 21st century high-tech know-how when it comes to eliminating the garbage in your life so that you can wake up and enjoy life each day. Indeed, The 72 Names of God is the ultimate pill for anything and everything that ails you because it strikes at the DNA level of your soul.

The power of The 72 Names of God operates strictly on a soul level, not a physical one. It's about spirituality, not religiosity. Rather than being limited by the differences that divide people, the wisdom of the Names transcends humanity's age-old quarrels and belief systems to deal with the one common bond that unifies all people and nations: the human soul.

True Prosperity

This is a revolution disguised as a book. Based on the secret tools and ancient wisdom of Kabbalah, the world's oldest science of truth, this new volume—by best-selling author Yehuda Berg—harnesses the ultimate truths of the universe as a tool for building prosperity. "Why is it that the people who make the most money out of so called money-making courses are the people who sell the courses?" Berg asks bluntly. "And why do people continue to struggle in anguish in a universe of abundance? And further: "Why do even those who achieve success do so at such bitter cost to their health, happiness, and well-being?" To answer each of these questions, Berg offers a radical overthrow of all our conventional notions of what constitutes money, success, prosperity—and reality! In *True Prosperity*, he launches a total system for achieving prosperity in every aspect of your life. You will learn, step by step, a new operating system for your life—how to become the boss and not the flunky in the business of your life. It is a methodology that you can apply every day and in every minute of your life, beginning now, to unlock the floodgates of money, happiness, fulfilling relationships . . . in a word, everything.

The Red String Book: The Power of Protection

Read the book that everyone is *wearing!*

Discover the ancient technology that empowers and fuels the hugely popular Red String, the most widely recognized tool of kabbalistic wisdom. Yehuda Berg, author of the international best-seller *The 72 Names of God: Technology for the Soul*, continues to reveal the secrets of the world's oldest and most powerful wisdom with his new book, *The Red String Book: The Power of Protection*. Discover the antidote to the negative effects of the dreaded "Evil Eye" in this second book of the Technology for the Soul series.

Find out the real power behind the Red String and why millions of people won't leave home without it.

It's all here. Everything you wanted to know about the Red String but were afraid to ask!

God Does Not Create Miracles. You Do!

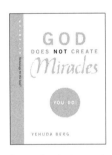

Stop "waiting for a miracle". . . and start making miracles happen!

If you think miracles are one-in-a-million "acts of God," this book will open your eyes and revolutionize your life, starting today! In *God Does Not Create Miracles*, Yehuda Berg gives you the tools to break free of whatever is standing between you and the complete happiness and fulfillment that is your real destiny.

You'll learn why entering the realm of miracles isn't a matter of waiting for a supernatural force to intervene on your behalf. It's about taking action now—using the powerful, practical tools of Kabbalah that Yehuda Berg has brought to the world in his international best sellers *The Power of*

Kabbalah and *The 72 Names of God*. Now Yehuda reveals the most astonishing secret of all: the actual formula for creating a connection with the true source of miracles that lies only within yourself.

Discover the Technology for the Soul that really makes miracles happen—and unleash that power to create exactly the life you want and deserve!

The Monster is Real: How to Face Your Fears and Eliminate Them Forever

What are you afraid of?

Just admit it! At this very moment, there's something (or maybe lots of things) that you're afraid of. No matter how convincing your fears may seem, this book will show you how to attack and defeat them at their most basic source. In *The Monster Is Real: How to Face Your Fears and Eliminate Them Forever*, Yehuda Berg, author of the international best-seller *The 72 Names of God*, reveals powerful, practical Kabbalistic tools for eliminating fear's inner causes once and for all. If fear in any form is bringing pain into your life, get ready for a hugely positive change. With *The Monster is Real*, another in the Technology for the Soul series, you'll learn how to conquer this age-old problem forever!

FOR TEENS

Life Rules

You're a teen. Pretty easy, right? All you've got is social pressure, academic pressure, family pressure, athletic pressure, financial pressure, romantic pressure, and pressure from the thing your biology teacher calls hormones.

And now we want to talk to you about spirituality?

Hang in there. This book isn't one more thing to feel pressured by. In fact, this book is about finding the pressure relief valve that's already built into your soul. And discovering how in the thick of suffering, or what may seem like suffering, you can find never-ending happiness and unlimited joy.

In *Life Rules*, Yehuda Berg distills the wisdom of Kabbalah into 13 steps that help you shift from being reactive (that's letting life do it to you) to being proactive (that's you doing it to life).

It's about embracing a spiritual path, but that's different from a religious path. Very different. You won't be shaving your head, giving up parties, or turning in your iPod. What you will be encouraged to do is jump even deeper into life: the fun, the scary, the comfortable, the uncomfortable, all of it. And embrace it.

Your natural state of being is what kabbalists call *Light-filled*—and through kabbalistic teachings made easy, personal experiences, and chapter exercises, *Life Rules* will gently challenge you to build the consciousness that will bring you back to this Light. When you do, you will tap into all the mind-blowing abundance and contentment you desire.

NEW FOR KIDS

The 72 Names of God for Kids:
A Treasury of Timeless Wisdom

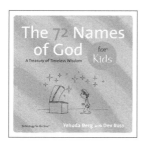

In often seemingly magical ways, the timeless philosophy portrayed in this book will help children overcome their fears and find their way to self-esteem, true friendship, love, and Light. The ancient secrets of Kabbalah revealed within these pages will give children a deeper understanding of their innate spiritual selves, along with powerful tools to help them make positive choices throughout their lives. The delightful, original color illustrations were created by the children of Spirituality for Kids who have used these universal lessons to change their own destinies. These are paired with simple and meaningful meditations, lessons, stories, poems, and fables inspired by the wisdom of Kabbalah.

MORE PRODUCTS THAT CAN HELP YOU BRING THE WISDOM OF KABBALAH INTO YOUR LIFE

God Wears Lipstick
By Karen Berg

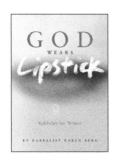

God Wears Lipstick is written exclusively for women (or for men who better want to understand women) by one of the driving forces behind the Kabbalah movement.

For thousands of years, women were banned from studying Kabbalah, the ancient source of wisdom that explains who we are and what our purpose is in this universe.

Karen Berg changed that. She opened the doors of The Kabbalah Centre to anyone who wanted to understand the wisdom of Kabbalah and brought Light to these people.

In *God Wears Lipstick*, Karen Berg shares that wisdom with us, especially as it affects you and your relationships. She reveals a woman's special place in the universe and why women have a spiritual advantage over men. She explains how to find your soulmate and your purpose in life. She empowers you to become a better human being as you connect to the Light, and she then gives you the tools for living and loving.

Becoming Like God
By Michael Berg

At the age of 16, kabbalistic scholar Michael Berg began the herculean task of translating *The Zohar*, Kabbalah's chief text, from its original Aramaic into its first complete English translation. *The Zohar*, which consists of 23 volumes, is considered a compendium of virtually all information pertaining to the universe, and its wisdom is only beginning to be verified today.

During the ten years he worked on *The Zohar*, Michael Berg discovered the long-lost secret for which humanity has searched for more than 5,000 years: how to achieve our ultimate destiny. *Becoming Like God* reveals the transformative method by which people can actually break free of what is called "ego nature" to achieve total joy and lasting life.

Berg puts forth the revolutionary idea that for the first time in history, an opportunity is being made available to humankind: an opportunity to Become Like God.

The Secret
By Michael Berg

Like a jewel that has been painstakingly cut and polished, *The Secret* reveals life's essence in its most concise and powerful form. Michael Berg begins by showing you how our everyday understanding of our purpose in the world is literally backwards. Whenever there is pain in our lives—indeed, whenever there is anything less than complete joy and fulfillment—this basic misunderstanding is the reason.

The Essential Zohar
By Rav Berg

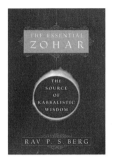

The Zohar has traditionally been known as the world's most esoteric and profound spiritual document, but Kabbalist Rav Berg, this generation's greatest living Kabbalist, has dedicated his life to making this wisdom universally available. The vast wisdom and Light of *The Zohar* came into being as a gift to all humanity, and *The Essential Zohar* at last explains this gift to the world.

The Power of You
By Rav Berg

For the past 5,000 years, neither science nor psychology has been able to solve the fundamental problem of chaos in people's lives.

Now, one man is providing the answer. He is Kabbalist Rav Berg.

Beneath the pain and chaos that disrupts our lives, Kabbalist Rav Berg brings to light a hidden realm of order, purpose, and unity. Revealed is a universe in which mind becomes master over matter—a world in which God, human thought, and the entire cosmos are mysteriously interconnected.

Join this generation's premier kabbalist on a mind-bending journey along the cutting edge of reality. Peer into the vast reservoir of spiritual wisdom that is Kabbalah, where the secrets of creation, life, and death have remained hidden for thousands of years.

Wheels of a Soul
By Rav Berg

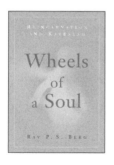

In *Wheels of a Soul*, Kabbalist Rav Berg reveals the keys to answering these and many more questions that lie at the heart of our existence as human beings. Specifically, Rav Berg explains why we must acknowledge and explore the lives we have already lived in order to understand the life we are living today . . .

Make no mistake: *you have been here before.* Reincarnation is a fact—and just as science is now beginning to recognize that time and space may be nothing but illusions, Rav Berg shows why death itself is the greatest illusion of all.

In this book you learn much more than the answers to these questions. You will understand your true purpose in the world and discover tools to identify your life's soul mate. Read *Wheels of a Soul* and let one of the greatest kabbalistic masters of our time change your life forever.

THE ZOHAR

"Bringing *The Zohar* from near oblivion to wide accessibility has taken many decades. It is an achievement of which we are truly proud and grateful."

—Michael Berg

Composed more than 2,000 years ago, *The Zohar* is a set of 23 books, a commentary on biblical and spiritual matters in the form of conversations among spiritual masters. But to describe *The Zohar* only in physical terms is greatly misleading. In truth, *The Zohar* is nothing less than a powerful tool for achieving the most important purposes of our lives.

It was given to all humankind by the Creator to bring us protection, to connect us with the Creator's Light, and ultimately to fulfill our birthright of true spiritual transformation.

More than eighty years ago, when The Kabbalah Centre was founded, *The Zohar* had virtually disappeared from the world. Few people in the general population had ever heard of it. Whoever sought to read it—in any country, in any language, at any price—faced a long and futile search.

Today all this has changed. Through the work of The Kabbalah Centre and the editorial efforts of Michael Berg, *The Zohar* is now being brought to the world, not only in the original Aramaic language but also in English.

The new English *Zohar* provides everything for connecting to this sacred text on all levels: the original Aramaic text for scanning; an English translation; and clear, concise commentary for study and learning.

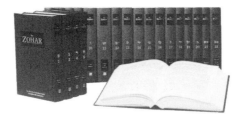

THE KABBALAH CENTRE

The International Leader in the Education of Kabbalah

Since its founding, The Kabbalah Centre has had a single mission: to improve and transform people's lives by bringing the power and wisdom of Kabbalah to all who wish to partake of it.

Through the lifelong efforts of kabbalists Rav and Karen Berg, and the great spiritual lineage of which they are a part, an astonishing 3.5 million people around the world have already been touched by the powerful teachings of Kabbalah. And each year, the numbers are growing!

I'd like to dedicate this book to all of us who at some time have felt like a victim of someone's behavior or hurtful words. Through the Light we access from the wisdom of this book, may we all find the power and the courage to take responsibility for our lives, find happiness, and help the world.

I'd also like to dedicate this book to The Kabbalah Centre for its guidance, inspiration, and empowerment. Without that, I would not be the same.

With love and light,

Tracey Nanula